Financial Cents

Making Sense out of your Cent$

by

Melanie J. Hicks

DORRANCE
PUBLISHING CO
EST. 1920
PITTSBURGH, PENNSYLVANIA 15238

Dorrance Publishing Co
585 Alpha Drive
Suite 103
Pittsburgh, PA 15238
Visit our website at www.dorrancebookstore.com

ISBN: 979-8-89211-094-5
eISBN: 979-8-89211-592-6

INTRODUCTION

Over the past 20 years, I have been to many financial seminars and listened to numerous prominent and also not so popular financial strategies of "money experts," but time after time I found their guides just didn't fit my situation. I found that, more often than not, I had to chew the meat and spit out the bones (even though I'm not a meat eater). This phrase simply means to use discernment and take in all available information but selectively distinguish the useful from the inapplicable. I've learned that everyone's financial recipe is not the same and everything is certainly not for everybody, but there is always a process out there just for you when it comes to the exchange of teaching and learning finances. Although this guide was carefully curated, it may make you feel the very same way I used to feel at the end of every financial seminar, and that is okay. It's important that you understand that you have to follow a financial recipe that works best for your situation. My goal is to simply help you make sense out of your cents.

As a single mother, there were many times when the only money I had to spare was literally cents, so for me I wasn't always able to make sense of how I could have my money work for me. Especially when so many "financial gurus" teach the key to financial stability and wealth is investing. When my oldest son was a young child, I was on the phone with a friend, and she told me I needed to open a 529 plan for my son. I was so frustrated and exclaimed to her, "How am I supposed to do that and I'm on public assistance? I'm trying to feed him, I don't have money to invest!" My displaced irritation was a result of my inability to make sense of my cents. At the time, I was in the beginning stages of learning the keys to financial management. As I continued to learn more, I thought I was doing something when my son was about five years old and a co-worker told me her fiancé was a financial advisor. So my plan was to start investing for my baby. I put $100 into an UTMA (Uniform Transfers to Minors Account) without a full understanding and let me tell you that $100 was about $1000 to me, because I was only making $12.40 an hour and parting with it was a true sacrifice. As time went on, I watched his account get swallowed by fees. Today, he has $10 in this account and that's only because the fee is more than $10. My son is an adult now and almost two decades later, I finally sat still after getting my degree from the dreaded "School of Hard Knocks" and realized that I wasn't spitting out enough bones or chewing enough meat. As you read on, I ask that you give this guide a try and take a bite. Take a moment to savor the flavor and see if it satisfies your financial pallet. Effective money management takes some sifting and slow chewing but eventually by chewing the meat and spitting out the bones you will get to the nutrients of your desired financial meal.

CHAPTER 1

The Power of the Penny

By the time I met with a financial advisor, I was already living on 125% of my paycheck. The advisor presented the 80/20 rule to me, and I realized that this was the start to avoid living paycheck to paycheck. The 80/20 rule simply means to set aside 10% of your income for giving, 10% should be set aside for you to pay yourself (invest), and the remaining 80% goes towards your living expenses. I gleaned this information and tried and tried to follow this rule but I kept failing. Why? It's because I was living on 125% of my check trying to look like the Jones's, metaphorically, all the while drowning figuratively. I wrote this book to share this information and hopefully help someone avoid making the same financial mistakes I made. I want to help you reduce the 125% to 80% and of course make sense out of your cents. Walk this financial journey out with me and let's take a look at the power of a penny.

Before I start digging into your pockets and purses, I want to share a nugget. In this day and age of cryptocurrency and debit cards I need you to understand as of right now there is still power in the penny. Yes, I am speaking of the little copper instrument that can make a difference in you completing a dollar or breaking a dollar. The very thing that when balancing your books makes you lose sleep if your books are off by one cent. There is power in the penny and the crazy part is it is the most disrespected type of currency. You can almost always find pennies on the ground when you are walking down the street. I know many people carelessly drop them, walk over them, and even dismiss them. Let me help you respect the power of the penny and view it a little differently.

What do I mean by respect? How is this possible? Well, respecting your finances means adding discipline to your routine and understanding every type of money counts toward building wealth. For instance, when you exercise, you only receive optimal results through discipline in your workout combined with your food management and water intake. The same applies to your money. The only way to see true results is if you combine respecting your money along with budgeting, giving, and knowing when to say "No." Keep reading and we'll get to those steps soon. The process of being disciplined isn't easy but I am here to show you that it's worth it.

When you find a penny or receive a penny in your change, respecting that penny helps you respect the process of gathering ninety-nine more pennies for a total of one dollar. Now add four more dollars to that one dollar and you have five dollars. Next, add three more five-dollar bills and now you have twenty dollars. We are on a roll. Keep going and add four more twenty-dollar bills to the one you already have and now you're at one hundred dollars. One day soon, when you reflect on the humble beginnings of your financial journey you will remember that it all started with one penny. Respect the power of the penny.

Challenge: Check your purses, couch, and car cushions for change. When you are walking and you see change on the ground (proceed with caution in areas that have drivers) gather the change, especially the pennies. See how fast you can get to $1.00 and then start all over again. Check with your financial institution to see if they will accept coins for dollars. If not, then take them to a change machine (be mindful of a fee). Finally, take your dollars and place them in your pay yourself account.

CHAPTER 2

The B Word: BUDGETING

Now that we know in order to make sense out of our cents we have to implement the 80/20 rule and value the power of the penny, we must now take a look at how we can make this happen in a practical way. It starts with the B word: Budgeting.

Budgeting can be done in different ways, and the good thing is there isn't only one way to budget. There are many budgeting tools from spreadsheets, pen and paper, phone applications, envelopes, planners, a check book registry, etc. There is no right tool to use as long as you choose one that best fits your lifestyle and work from there. On the road to financial improvement, we buy books and go to seminars searching for the special formula to budgeting and all along the special formula to budgeting is purely discipline and knowing where your money is going. Now let me be clear, budgeting was and still isn't my strong suit, but I continue to budget because I know my discipline will help me reach my long-term financial goals.

For me, a majority of the time the bills were more than the money, and I would often walk away after my budget spreadsheet just didn't balance. To tell the truth I would say "God, you see this, I need your help." We may not have always had what we wanted but our needs were always met. Nothing was ever shut off and we consistently had food and clothes. Maybe not the food that made you smack your fingers and rub your belly in complete satisfaction or the latest and greatest clothes, but the necessities were covered.

I remember one time I had $10.00, and I needed gas in the car, but we also needed groceries. I had some food in the house, but you know sometimes you have part of the ingredients, like peanut butter but no bread. Well, let me tell you, after working all day the last thing I possessed was creativity in the kitchen. I took that $10.00 and bought half a pizza and called off from work the next day to save gas from driving (this was before remote working was a thing). We made it to the following day which was a pay day, so I could get some gas and shop for groceries to stretch for two weeks. Like many Americans, I made too much money to get government assistance but not enough to last for the biweekly pay periods. I was no longer working for the automotive industry which meant taking a $40,000 pay cut when I transitioned to corporate America. My starting pay was $28,000 with two children, a mortgage, and a car note. Due to my extreme change of income, budgeting became a major part of my life. How did I figure it out? I stopped trying to please the masses and began to watch what I spent and I stopped letting others spend my money. What do I mean by "others spending my money"? People often mean well, especially those close to you. Sometimes our friends or family will say, "You should buy this or that," and it sounds good at the time, but when the light bill and gas bill is due, where are the **"you should"** people to help you pay the bills?

Spreadsheets are my favorite budgeting method even though the thought alone can be daunting to some. With a spreadsheet, you can preset your specific expenses to track where all your income for the month will be used. You can automatically deduct the 10% for giving and 10% to pay yourself. Then you can set calculations to tally how much your monthly expenses are and if they meet or exceed the 80%. By doing this, you can determine if you have a zero balance, a deficit, or a surplus to carry over to the next month.

Another practical budgeting method is the envelope method. Instead of direct deposit, cash your checks and label your envelopes according to your expenses. For example, title your envelopes under the following names, "giving," "saving," "expenses," and if you choose to treat yourself that money should come from the "pay yourself" funds. Be sure to break down your expenses into subcategories, the monthly utilities, food, gas for your car, etc. Once the expenses envelope is empty, you are done until the next paycheck. There is something about feeling the currency leave your hands that keeps you alert and on track with budgeting.

A third example is plain old pen and paper, this budgeting strategy will never get old. When you write down what your expenses are and how much you can save and how much you can give, it does something to your mindset about being very careful about splurging on needs and wants. Don't get discouraged when you first try one of these methods. Keep in mind discipline is the hidden formula for successful budgeting.

Challenge: Choose the method that works best for you and work with it. You may have to do a few trial-and-error moments and that's perfectly fine. When you find the one or two that works best for you begin the process and begin to build your financial muscles.

The You Should People

Let's talk about the "you should" people. Who are these people in our lives? Well, we all have "you should" people in our lives, and if you can't think of any one, you may be the "you should" person to those in your life. So who are these people? Sometimes it's your bestie who means you no harm, and will see some shoes or a purse that is so you and encourage you to purchase the amazing glittery images for instant gratification, but when the bills are due crickets enter the space they once were standing. Now don't get me wrong, the "you should" people can also be productive life assets. I'm a "you should" person as a mom in the life of my sons (so I think). Their eyes gloss over when my sentence starts with "I was thinking maybe YOU SHOULD..." My youngest told me see this is why I don't tell you about my finances, because you want to spend it. I see myself as suggesting financial guidance as most "you should" people think they are providing, but at the end of the day "Don't let nobody spend your money, honey." Be wise in your decisions and the "you should" people may become the "I SHOULD HAVE..." people, after watching you navigate this financial journey.

Nugget: Don't let anyone spend "***Your money, honey.***"

Chapter 3
Just Say NO

The word "No" is defined as a negative expression, and quite frankly no matter how kindly it is used, something about using and hearing the word always stings. Over time I've learned the difference between a "Hard No" as opposed to a "harsh No?" Now what do I mean by a hash "No?" Well, say if your child asked you if you think they are capable of accomplishing their dream of being a rapper? Astronaut? Dancer? Dinosaur? And you say "no." That's harsh. Why? Because that is a dream that helps them to imagine bigger and greater and beyond the stars. When your child asks you for a $900.00 coat or a $300.00 pair of sneakers that "no" can be hard. Doesn't matter if you can afford it. Is that a value-added asset or a fashion statement that is fleeting? While growing up, hearing the word "no" wasn't uncommon. My mom didn't enjoy saying "No" to her only daughter, but it was something I needed growing up in the 70s and 80s. For example, I grew up in a time when designer jeans were the new thing, and there was one brand I really wanted to wear. My little friends had them, and I wanted a pair so badly. I remember asking my mother for a pair of the special brand of jeans, and she said "NO!" point blank, period. The exact quote was, "They don't pay me to wear their label on my behind!" Well, my little world was shattered, so I thought. Fast forward to my adulthood, now I'm buying my own clothes and I find myself saying, "They aren't paying me to wear or carry their labels." I live by the slogan, "If it's free, it's for me," otherwise I make my purchases based on quality and affordability. As a result, I am not drowning in debt trying to keep up with the Jones's by making purchases based solely on the name of a label.

I remember telling my mom I was going to a branch in the military. Let me tell you that was a harsh "no," and she had a few choice words that followed behind it… My mom loves the armed forces; my brother and uncles and aunts were members, she just wasn't seeing it for me.

Prior to having children, I remember saying, "I won't tell my children 'no' when I get older." Yes, I sure did utter one of those, "I will never say that to my kid" sentences, and let me tell you I didn't just repeat the sentence; I could hear my mother's voice as I was forming the words. When my boys were growing up, "No" was almost a curse word to most of their friends. Their friends seemed to be a little more privileged as they always had the latest sneakers, video games, clothes, etc. On the other hand, I was struggling to keep the lights on and food on the table. One thing for sure, we weren't going to be able to eat off those sneakers. Whenever I told my oldest child "No," he would walk away and take the "No" as law. Keep in mind he really didn't ask for much so I didn't have to say "no" often to him. I'm sure he didn't like hearing it, but he rolled with it. My youngest child, please, let me exhale first. Whew. I had to turn into my mother with this one. He asked for everything! Don't get me wrong, his dad would get him some of the things but asking for $$$ pricey sneakers when we have a $$$ pricey gas bill just made that "hard NO" my word of the day. I told my son he can get the expensive shoes, but he would need to get a job. Those hard no's instilled a deep work ethic in my boys. At a young age, they understood if they wanted something bad enough they would need to work for it. My youngest son started working at 15 years old at his best friend's family business to get money for whatever he wanted and he even purchased his first car at 17 years old. My oldest son cut our neighbor's grass, sold home-made cookies to his friends, and worked at a tire plant one summer with his friends at the referral of my brother, his uncle, and stacked to buy his first car.

Parenting is a lot different now and as parents we often want our children to have what we didn't have growing up so we avoid "No's" which can sometimes come with a hefty price tag. The short but powerful two letter word can save your wallet as well as your child's life. You may be wondering, "How can telling your child 'No' save their life?"

When I state it will save their lives, as I've stated before a hard "No" from you will sting, hurt their feelings, but that very "No" from someone else won't hit as hard. The "No" of a stranger just means that door wasn't for them to walk through and it's water off a duck's back. Your "No" should be colored with love. Some of that old school parenting kept us alive, and as we matured we discovered some of those "no's" also viewed as closed doors were actually blessings for something greater. I reflect on the hard "no's" and how they prepared me to understand that not everything I wanted was meant to be mines. I wanted to go in a career direction of medicine to be a doctor but the closed doors and the hard No's" directed to me to my God-given talent of finance and all it has to offer. The "No's" hurt me along the way but built my character. The hard "No's" will build character in your child.

Challenge: Take time to reflect and think about your "No" pattern when it comes to you and your children. How do your "No's" compare to your wallet? Is there anything you can say "no" to today that will help you save money to invest?

Chapter 4

No Spend Month

Now if you're anything like me, you're probably looking at this title sideways and questioning, "How am I supposed to not spend any money for a WHOLE month with little mouths to feed?" There were many times when I personally didn't have any extra money after all the necessary bills were paid so I understand how this title could be viewed as off-putting. You are justified in viewing this concept sideways and wondering if I've completely lost it, but let me explain. Necessities always come first so thoroughly review all your expenses during your budget review. Pay your regular monthly recurring bills such as food, light, gas for the house and vehicle, mortgage/rent, water bill, car note, life/medical insurance. If you have anything left over put it aside and do not spend it for one whole month.

Instead, let's do some research and get creative. It's time to head to YouTube University and learn how to do your own hair, polish your nails and toes, make your own coffee, etc. for this month. Many cities have websites that list free activities each week. Check your town's website to see what is happening in your area. Look for activities and events that you can even walk to within your community. How about taking the children to the local park or the school playground? I dare you to even disconnect from the phone and just hang out with them and be a big kid yourself.

I live in a city where cold weather is normally in the forecast so if you live in a place like I do, well then, go indoors and take a trip to the closest library, and get a library card for you and the kiddos to utilize your local library's resources. Reading can be fun and a learning experience at the same time. Having friends with children the same age can allow for play dates and grown-up conversations at each others' homes. There is something special about face-to-face interaction. If it's a nice day outside, go for a walk. I remember my sons and I walking around our neighborhood admiring our neighbors' homes and beautiful trees. This is not only free and a way to spend to time in the community, but it allows your child to become acquainted with their surroundings, teaching them to recognize landmarks, and it gives them space to tell you about their day while walking or bike riding in your own community.

A no spend month is not intended to be a punishment; instead it is designed to help you avoid staying in a place of frivolous spending and to become more conscientious about your purchases. This is why it's important to entertain yourself and especially the kids with something you can do for free so you don't feel imprisoned by your discipline.

Challenge: This will be a two-part challenge. First, start with no spending for a week. Seems possible right? Next try two weeks, then three, and finally try to avoid additional spending for one month. How much have you saved? Next, look on your town's website or your local newspaper for free events/activities. All this information can also be accessed at your local library for free as well.

Chapter 5

Cook What You Already Have Available

I am a Buffalonian, true blue through and through. We've survived countless winter storms and blizzards, needless to say we are built for snow days. A major part of any natural storm preparedness is ensuring you have enough essentials such as food, water, and battery-operated lights. I do not currently eat meat so it has been customary for me to maintain a stash of canned and packaged foods. In 2016, during a family trip to Aruba I decided to slightly change my eating habits and opted to give up meats after I completely recovered from the treatments of Stage Two breast cancer in 2014. Whereas, when it came to my sons, the concept of giving up meat, was a hard "NO!" Fast forward to the COVID pandemic, I stored enough food staples such as beans, rice, and canned vegetables. More recently, Buffalo was expecting yet another winter snowstorm so on the day before landfall was expected, I went to the store to get nacho chips and cookies (I said I changed my eating habits slightly). The snow fell and the wind blew and blew and it snowed more and the wind blew harder to where you couldn't see the house across the street. Leaving the house for more groceries or ordering takeout was impossible at this point. I looked through my cabinets, freezer, and refrigerator and bit my lip.

During this winter storm, I was so blessed to wake up in the house with both of my adult sons home on this particular stormy Christmas weekend. Why is that a surprise? Well, because they are grown and living their best lives so the last place they may be is at home with Mom on a holiday weekend. The Christmas festivities that were to be held at my mother's home were canceled due to the storm, and I was now in the house with two grown men who were still consumers of meats, and again I don't eat or buy meat normally. I searched the freezer and found hash browns and apple chicken sausage. Now let me start this by saying I have no idea when I bought this stuff. I also had a bag of fresh potatoes and I always try to keep onions. So I got creative and made them freezer-burned sausage and hash browns with potatoes and onions. Don't judge me. They ate but there is always one in the crowd that complains and then tells you "no offense to you (the cook)." My youngest went through the fridge on his cell phone, video chatting with his cousin, and was yelling, "All we have is vegetables, vegetables, and more vegetables." Now in my head I'm thinking this young person has such major first-world issues. However, I'm going to be honest with you, by day three of the storm I was saying the same thing: "vegetables, vegetables, vegetables, ugh!" My god sister once said, "If you look at a person's wallet (meaning their spending habits) you will see where their heart is." Well, my heart was at a local grocery store desiring more chocolate chip cookies. Don't get me wrong, I can make some plant-based chocolate chip walnut cookies, but I can't make them like my family in Florida makes them, so when grocery shopping, find a balance. Don't go so hard in the healthy only side or processed food only side. Do your best to find a middle ground so you have the food you need but also the foods you enjoy. Try this Challenge below and see where your wallet and heart stand.

Challenge: How many meals can you make from what you already have in the refrigerator and kitchen cabinets? Use this week to meal prep and be sure to create a balanced grocery list with what you need and also what you enjoy.

CHAPTER 6

Financial Giving

"And a poor widow came and put in two small copper coins, which make a penny.

And he called his disciples to him and said to them, "Truly, I say to you, this poor widow has put in more than all those who are contributing to the offering box. For they all contributed out of their abundance, but she out of her poverty has put in everything she had, all she had to live on." Mark 12:42–44

I referenced the above scripture because it shows when you give with humility attached to it, God will always recognize a giving heart and begin to open doors and windows. Let me tell you a story about giving. I was working in the automotive industry making really good money, spoiling my sons, and living a good life. Well, at the time I was in a relationship and was able to travel with the kids plus cover all of my normal expenses such as mortgage, car note, groceries, etc. I was living my best life, well, or so I thought because I was giving my tithes and offerings to the church, and the person I was dating at the time didn't give to the church and he was still being blessed. So over time my money got a little tight because life happens, and I decided, well, if he doesn't give and is being blessed why am I still giving? So I decided to stop giving to the church and all my money began to disappear. I chose to be selfish with my money and only spend it on me and my house instead of giving God my first fruits. Well, let me tell you, my selfish act was short lived. I hurried and began to give again, and it seemed as if my pockets stopped having holes in them. Make giving a part of your routine. I know you're probably asking how giving will help improve your financial situation? Sometimes the process of giving your way out of debt doesn't always make sense but it works. Just know that wasn't the first or last time I tried not giving and the results were always the same.

Another time, I wasn't a member of any church mainly because of church hurt and life decisions, but I was still putting my 10% aside because of the lessons I had learned in the School of Hard Knocks. I remember praying and asking God where do you want me to give this money? I kept seeing a specific not-for-profit organization being advertised every time I would wake up in the middle of the night. I gathered the money and went to the organization. This was August of 2006 and I asked if I could donate the money, and oddly enough it was a struggle trying to get them to take the money. I was beginning to wonder if I was being punked but eventually they took the money. I walked out frustrated and relieved at the same time. I'm so happy I gave the donation because October of 2006 we had the storm of the century in Buffalo. My house never lost power, and I went from a household of 3 to a household of 11 people comfortably as family members came to stay with us. We never ran out of food, we never lost power, and I can truly say it was fun. When it was all said and done, I was reminded in my spirit of the giving and how God always shows up on time. Will your experience be just like mine? Probably not; it may be even better as God is no respecter of persons. I just want to impress how giving is essential. I remember listening to a well-known minister on television one day, and he said when things got tight financially him and his wife would sit together and see where they could give, and God would always open the windows of heaven.

Challenge: Start giving, even if it is a small amount. There is joy, peace, and humility in giving. There will always be sowing and reaping seasons. The promise is what you sow, you shall reap. Give it a try. It's easy for some and challenging for others. When you practice a discipline, it gets easier and easier. Flex your giving muscle. Give your way into wealth.

Chapter 7

Non Financial Giving

For God so loved the world that He gave His only begotten Son, that whoever believes in Him should not perish but have everlasting life. John 3:16

We can never beat God's giving, no matter how hard we may try. As you work through the budgeting and 80/20 process, I want you try to strive to give. Sometimes we have so much stuff we don't need or items we can no longer use; we simply need to release it. I remember one time I heard the Lord tell me to clean out my closet. I didn't challenge it because I was in a stage of transition. So I went through the process of cleaning out my closet and donated tons of clothes, then I looked at my closet and realized I was lacking dresses. I spoke a word out loud in my private space and within a week Auntie, who had no clue I had done this, began to send me boxes of dresses from North Carolina where she was living. The funny part was I was asked by co-workers where I got my clothes from, and I would respond, "My aunt sends them to me" and the response would be, "Well, you just could have told me you didn't want me to know where you shopped." I would laugh so hard, because little did they know, I didn't shop for many years.

Due to my obedience, the blessings overflowed. God later told me to give away my purses and shoes, and I loved purses, shoes, and sneakers. I had a friend who had a business that specialized in helping women dress for success. I donated my shoes and some of the purses and then I gave the other purses to some other organizations. Well, let me tell you, Auntie called me and said, "I have some purses if you want them?" Of course my answer was "Yes," because she only purchased high quality items, especially purses. Now when it came to my shoes, me and God had to have a conversation, because my shoe game restoration is still in slow recovery. I realized it's because I placed most of my value in those things.

The biggest non-financial give for me was when God had me give away my truck. I had come to the realization that when we purge and allow him in, we soar, and the windows of heaven open up. My 2010 Equinox SUV was paid off and only had 57,000 miles on it and we were in 2016. I had just bought some new tires, and I told God and myself I was going to drive this truck until the wheels fall off. My dream car was a RX350 Lexus, but I told myself this Equinox is my Lexus. One Friday morning on my way to work I heard a clear audible voice telling me to give my car to my cousin. I was in disbelief. I kept saying "Is this me?" I am nice but I'm not that nice to GIVE away my paid-off vehicle. I arrived at work feeling numb. I logged into my computer and the rest of the day was a blur until that evening. I remember my Auntie calling me, asking me to take her somewhere on that Saturday. Well, I was all in my feelings and told her, "Tomorrow is my Sabbath, and I have to see what God says." She replied, "Okay." Crazy, right? She was asking me to assist her, and I'm saying, "Let me see what God says." I went driving that night crying and asking God if he was going to make me ride the bus. You know God has a sense of humor.

Unbeknownst to me, my cousin was praying to God asking him to bless her with a car. He was working behind the scenes, but neither of us knew how or through who.

Once Saturday arrived, I called my aunt and asked her if she wanted to take a walk. I picked her up and drove to our local park, and as we walked, I told her God told me to give my car away, but I didn't disclose to whom. Well, when God does a thing in private, he reveals it. My Auntie casually said, "Oh he said give it to…" who is one of my cousins. I burst out crying like she had slapped me in the face. She proceeded to explain that God can't give us a new thing when we're holding on to the old. We completed the walk and went to my house, and it just so happened Prima was driving around the corner to my house. I saw my cousin, and she was in a bit of a hurry it seemed. I asked her if she liked my car and she said, "It's okay." I looked up and said, "God, umm, I'll do it again." I asked her again, "What do you think of my car?" She replied, "Why are you asking me what do I think of your car when I don't have a car?" I looked at her and took a deep exhale because of her response, and then I explained to her, "God told me to give you my car." She was in awe and shared that she was just praying for God to help her get a car. She asked me if she could give me something for it. I began to think, well I did just buy tires and my Auntie immediately said, "Melanie!!!!" I responded to her question with a quiet and reluctant "No" with my head held low.

Fast forward to Monday, I dropped off my car to her house and picked up my Lexus RX350 fresh off the lot. I said all of that to say when God tells you to give, do it because obedience is greater than sacrifice. God wants to bless us, but we hold up the blessings with clutter and when we clean it out the blessings flow.

Challenge: Spend a weekend de-cluttering your home. What are you holding onto that no longer serves you? Give gently used items away. Find a family, local church, or donation organization that can help distribute the items.

CHAPTER 8

Saving

To be the most transparent that I can be has been another area of struggle for me. I would attempt to save, and life would begin to start happening. I wasn't disciplined and it took time and practice. The kids always needed something, and if it wasn't them it was the car and/or the house. There would be people in my inner circle checking my pockets and trying to spend my money. Just saying NO works on those who want to spend your money, honey. My lack of discipline continued to rear its head until I found my best way to budget. I had to go through numerous processes until I found my niche. I would put the bills and everything first, and I would be left with nothing until I learned to walk out a "no spend month" with coupons (physical and digital). This helped with cutting costs, but not skimping on quality. I remember shopping at this one store for groceries that required me to pack my own bags or using empty boxes, and I was being talked about for being cheap. Well, I see people driving Mercedes Benz and Lincolns in the parking lot shopping at this store now. Saving money to save their budgets.

Changing how I grocery shopped and cooked helped me save money. I began to shop for my beans and spices from the ethnic stores. When I cook, I will peel the onions and garlic and peppers, carrots, and mushroom tips, and I will take the scraps and put them in the freezer. When the bag gets full, I will boil the scraps and make veggie broth and freeze that for future use. Then I would attempt to compost the boiled scraps in my yard for a garden (you see I specified "attempt"). I'm still working on that discipline but at least now I don't feel as if I'm tossing money out. This makes me feel one step closer to saving. You might save 2–4 dollars just making your own veggie broth. The power of the penny can have you changing 2–4 dollars a month to 24–48 a year if you use broth once a month.

With your savings you've accumulated from better budgeting and the no spend month, open up an online savings account with a high interest if possible. So when life happens and you find that you're going over the 80 percent you are able to reach back if needed for emergencies. Strive to put at least $1,200 in the "Stuff be happening" account and keep it liquid. With a portion of this account, you can look to begin to invest. The pay yourself savings account can help you begin to build wealth and accumulate assets.

Investing

Let me first preface this topic with I am not a financial advisor, or financial fiduciary nor do I give out investing advice. I will say that investing can help line up with your savings plans. Read some of my mishaps and the journey I took and am still on when it comes to properly investing. I just wanted to share some of my pit falls like I referenced earlier about the UTMA account for my oldest son. I was trying this thing out with little knowledge and word of mouth references. References are great for getting a new doctor or trying out a restaurant, but when it comes to your dollar, research and self-education is the best route. I took the route many of us take when we don't know something: word of mouth referral of a financial advisor. So I had accumulated a few dollars and bought mutual funds for my sons. I had spent $250.00 apiece (this was before you could buy fractional pieces of stock like we can today). I was so excited and the mutual funds had Disney as one of the stocks within. I had just invested for my sons, and I was going to start the wealth legacy. I had gone to a financial advisor and trusted this was going to grow as they grew. Well, life happens and less than six months later I needed to cash them out. Life was happening and the disappointment I felt was indescribable. What I can say is I never stopped trying and falling. Those falls were lessons and taxable ouches because they were short term, which hold a penalty I wasn't aware of as opposed to long term holdings, but tax talk is for another day and time. Well, the interesting part was I sent my mom to this person and because we hadn't invested millions, we were low on the totem poll of financial care and it showed. My mom's money she invested dwindled away and let me tell you, I hear about it every time we speak on investing. My mom was one and done, she was left with a bad taste from this experience. I know that there are amazing advisors out there because I have encountered many, but I had to learn some things for myself when it came to the process of investing. What I learned was not to just go on verbal reference, do the due diligence for yourself. Some financial professionals are looking at the commission they will receive and not the returns that may be best for your investment. I recommend this book by Tony Robbins, *Money: Master the Game*. This book became a game changer for me on how I viewed investments and financial professionals.

One of my other learned lessons, and let me say again I am not advising, but when I had found myself drowning in debt as a single income household, and I had more months than money. I did take out a loan against my 401k account with my employer. The loan allowed me to pay off debt as well as pay myself back at a specific interest rate, while still paying into the 401k. There were certain questions I had to ask myself:

Can I afford to pay myself back?

How long of a payment cycle do I want? 36 months? 48 months? 60 months? This question is super important. Why? Because in the beginning you may be okay with the payment but about halfway through, sometimes we forget what we were paying for, and it becomes a burden instead of a blessing.

Challenge: Check your level of discipline. Are you just spending your left-over money, or are you saving and paying yourself? Slow and steady wins the race. You don't have to rush because sometimes that builds pressure and frustration. Create a savings account that you can place the money and begin to build assets instead of buying liabilities.

CHAPTER 9

Married Ladies: Let's Talk Money, Honey

Now a wife of one of the prophets appealed to Elisha for help, saying, "Your servant, my husband is dead. You know that your servant was a loyal follower of the LORD. Now the creditor is coming to take away my two boys to be his servants." 2 Kings 4:1 https://www.biblegateway.com/passage *NLT (New English Translation)*

When I was laying in the bed one day during the last 2022 winter storm, God spoke to my spirit for the married ladies. He said, "the widow and the two sons." You know sometimes having a conversation with the Lord becomes a research event. I looked it up, then God blessed me to bring it to you this way: The man of God was taking care of his family, his beautiful wife, his awesome sons. It seemed as if life was amazing. In marriage, we often take on roles. You know, "I'll do this, and you take care of that." Back then, men primarily worked and managed the money while women took care of the home. Assigned roles work well until tragedy happens, such as a spouse becomes ill, loss of income, or even worse, death. The death of her husband has completely turned her life upside down.

I pondered about this story and wanted to view this story in modern times. I had many questions: Did they sit down and discuss the finances together? Or did he just handle it all? Was there a life insurance policy in place? Were his and her spending habits out of control to where his income or their incomes couldn't handle the change, but it was never discussed? Were they living above their means? Did he lose his job and the past bills took over? There are so many scenarios that can extend from this one passage and so many thoughts can run through your mind, reminding us just how important it is to discuss finances with our spouse. Come together and discuss all things financial. Are you all giving, donating? Are all the bills paid on time? What are your savings looking like? "Life be lifin,'" rainy day, sunshiny day whatever you want to name the account? Are you able to live within 80% of the net, or do you all need to cut back on some things together as a partnership? Are you both sacrificing some wants for financial security?

I can't just end there, we have to walk this scripture out because of the miracles, signs, and wonders revealed in the text. The amazing part is the widow knew who to turn to. She appealed to Elisha and at first he asked, "What do you want me to do?" Sometimes we have to just speak the thing. There is power in words so watch your words (that's a word for another time, I'm just saying). Next, Elisha asked the woman about what she already had in her house? (Look, we all know God can do much with little, we just have to have faith). Elisha advised the woman to reach out to the neighbors for some vessels. Specifically, all the containers she could get her hands on (sometimes you need to borrow a tool or two from the neighbors to get your house in order). This final part is mind-blowing. Elisha stated, "Go and shut your door behind you" (God will bless you openly but it's the work you do in private behind closed doors that show great reward). He told her to take the little oil she had to fill up all the vessels. She poured and poured and poured until all the containers were full and then the oil stopped. She invested behind closed doors and the abundance came to where she was able to pay all her debt and still have a profit left over. Seek God in all you do, even in your finances.

Challenge: Sit down with your spouse and talk it out. Make it a cute fun event with a nice dinner at home (not during game time). Light some candles, sit next to each other like you are about to be in the sheets, except it will be with spreadsheets. Have an amazing dessert ready when it's all done. Finances can be frustrating or fun. Let's make it fun.

CHAPTER 10

Credit From Friend to Foe to Friend Again

The word credit may bring numerous thoughts to our minds, depending on where we are in life and our experience or inexperience with credit. When I was younger, one of the dopest things my mother ever did was list me as an authorized user on her credit card.

However, she didn't talk to me about how dangerous having a credit card could be if you're not careful with it. I'm not blaming my mother at all. What she did was awesome because I didn't even know parents were able to do this to help jump start credit building (she was so ahead of her time). Don't get it twisted. Although she gave me the card she definitely let me know the purchases I made were the ones I was responsible to pay off. I really think my mom should have been a teacher since she was always trying to give me and my brother teachable life lessons.

Since my mom placed me on one of her retail credit cards, I was super responsible because it was under her name. On the other hand, as a college student who thinks they know everything already, I wanted my independence. I opened my own retail credit card from another well-known retailer at the time and let me tell you, I went shopping crazy. I would go to school in one outfit, and if my mom let me take the car to school, I would go to the mall on the way home to buy another outfit to go to work in simply because I was over the outfit I was already wearing that day. I was able to manage and keep up with my credit card bills until I had my oldest son. New expenses came rolling in and old bills were lingering. I eventually had to go to consumer credit counseling to get back on track.

My mother's intentions were great, but I was not knowledgeable or prepared enough for a credit card. Credit was indeed my foe. Let's talk about it. Good credit comes in handy when you're looking to buy a house or a car. You may ask, well what about those who use credit to buy groceries because they have more mouths than money. What about when life be lifing, and you need gas in your car to travel back and forth to work and you can't even scrounge up enough couch cushion change. To be honest, with today's gas prices, couch cushion change better come in the form of dollars. I had to make some tough decisions for credit to become my friend again.

I learned to try not to use credit on things that will perish quicker than it can be paid off. What do I mean by this? I learned not to use my major credit card on things I won't be able to see or use within three months. For example, gas in my car or groceries for the week. I also tried not to use my retail cards unless they were really needed for school clothes shopping during a growth spurt. Honestly, by the time I would have attempted to pay that bill off they would have outgrown the clothes again. One time my youngest son came home and told me a kid was calling him a bum because his pants were too short, and it broke my heart. I took him to the mall ASAP and overdrew my account. By buying him new clothes and utilizing my overdraft protection line of credit, I was charged a fee for the withdrawal in addition to interest for the purchase.

Once I finally paid off that line of credit I made the decision to unlink the credit card from my account. I realized I became dependent upon it instead of monitoring my coins. Once I did that my frivolous spending minimized. Now when I spend I keep a running calculation of purchases in my head then I settle my accounts by reviewing my purchases and applying them to my financial spreadsheet. Did I overdraw my account again? Yes, a few times because of forgotten purchases. I learned to use my phone calculator while I'm out shopping and tallying my purchases as I go along to help me get better with my budgeting and putting my cards away unless I really needed them.

To the parents with good credit, think about putting your child on your credit card, except don't physically give them the card. Check the age limit for authorized users. Some card companies don't have an age limit. The earlier you start building your child's credit while keeping your credit intact you can set your child up for success. This simple step will allow your child to begin to build their credit history. As a result, you won't have to co-sign for their future purchases. Discuss credit options such as interest rates and the difference between retail and major credit cards with your children. Knowledge is power, and it's important to keep credit as a friend while teaching your children to do the same.

Just like my mother, I also put both of my sons on my credit cards as authorized users and provided them the card. They have proven to be financially responsible with the cards I've given them. Once my oldest son's card expired, I didn't give it back to him because he had enough history to get his own card and car. My youngest is still using the card, and I haven't had to co-sign for his purchase of a car. The best thing to do is to plan to keep the card open and use it to buy dinner or lunch once every six months to keep it active.

Challenge: Go to www.annualcreditreport.com for your FREE annual credit report once a year to make sure there aren't any mistakes on your report that you may need to dispute. You can also check to see if your financial institution or your credit card company offers you access to your FICO score for free.

Glossary

What is a UTMA?

UTMA—Uniform Transfers Minor Account—refers to a law that allows a minor to receive gifts without the aid of a guardian or trustee. Gifts can include money, patents, royalties, real estate, and fine art.

A UTMA account allows the gift giver or an appointed custodian to manage the minor's account until the latter is of age. It also shields the minor from tax consequences on the gifts, up to a specified value.

https://www.investopedia.com/terms/u/utma.asp#t oc-what-is-the-uniform-transfers-to-minors-act-utma

What is finance fiduciary?

A fiduciary has an obligation to act in the best interests of another party. A fiduciary investment adviser is obligated to choose investment products that are in the best interests of the client regardless of self-interest or a third party's interests.

https://www.investopedia.com/financial-edge/0912/5-misconceptions-about-a-fiduciary.aspx#:~:text=A%20fiduciary%20has%20an%20obligation,or%20a%20third%20party's%20interests.

What Is a Financial Advisor?

A financial advisor helps people create long-term strategies for building wealth and managing risk. They can help you track, manage, and balance your investment portfolio. They can also provide helpful advice on lots of other financial issues and decisions.

Here's the gist of it: Financial advisors help you with all types of financial planning. This means everything from saving for retirement to handling an inheritance. The best advisors break down confusing financial jargon in ways you can understand. And they'll work with you—as a partner—to make a game plan that puts you on track to achieve your financial goals and retirement dreams.

https://www.ramseysolutions.com/retirement/what-does-a-financial-advisor-do

What is a Mutual Fund?

Mutual funds let you pool your money with other investors to "mutually" buy stocks, bonds, and other investments.

They're run by professional money managers who decide which securities to buy (stocks, bonds, etc.) and when to sell them.

You get exposure to all the investments in the fund and any income they generate.

They offer a wide variety of investment strategies and styles.

https://www.schwab.com/mutual-funds/under-stand-mutual-funds#panel—66-long-94941

What Is a 401(k) Plan?

A 401(k) plan is a retirement savings plan offered by many American employers that has tax advantages for the saver. It is named after a section of the U.S. Internal Revenue Code (IRC).

(IRC) Office of the Law Revision Counsel. U.S. Code: 26 USC 401: Qualified Pension, Profit-sharing, and Stock Bonus Plans.

https://www.investopedia.com/terms/1/401kplan.asp

What is the meaning of interest rate?

What is an interest rate? The interest rate is the amount a lender charges a borrower and is a percentage of the principal—the amount loaned. The interest rate on a loan is typically noted on an annual basis known as the annual percentage rate (APR).

https://www.investopedia.com/terms/i/interestrate.asp#:~:text=Investopedia%20%2F%20Julie%20Bang-,What%20Is%20an%20Interest%20Rate%3F,annual%20percentage%20rate%20(APR).

What is a 529 Plan?

A 529 plan is an investment account that offers tax benefits when used to pay for qualified education expenses for a designated beneficiary. You can use a 529 plan to pay for college, K-12 tuition, apprenticeship programs, and even student loan repayments. If using a 529 plan to save for college, your savings will have a minimal impact on financial aid eligibility.

https://www.savingforcollege.com/intro-to-529s/what-is-a-529-plan

What does FICO stand for? And what is a FICO score?

The Fair Isaac Corporation

A FICO Score is a three-digit number based on the information in your credit reports. It helps lenders determine how likely you are to repay a loan. This, in turn, affects how much you can borrow, how many months you have to repay, and how much it will cost (the interest rate).

https://www.myfico.com/credit-education/what-is-a-fico-score

The Author

The author Melanie J. Hicks, at the age of four years old, while under the care of her maternal grandmother, asked, "Do I have bank account?" Little did the author know that question would begin her observation of human behavior and their finances.

Melanie is the mother of two sons and a grandmother. She completed her Bachelor in Science in 2011 with a focus in accounting and her Masters in Science in 2014 global business with a focus in accounting from Daemen University, all while working full-time. After completing her degree in August of 2014, Melanie was diagnosed with breast cancer in October of 2014, and as a single mother of two she quickly realized her finances would be affected. Melanie purposed in her heart that she would take the lessons she had learned along the way to survivorship, and share them with women on how to manage in a financial crisis.

Nugget: It took the author 11 years to complete her bachelor's degree; her youngest was six months when she started the journey and 11 years old when she completed the degree. The author shared this tidbit, because she wanted to let you know hold on to your dreams and persevere no matter how long it takes, keep going.